Easy Peasy

D1487472

Easy Bake Oven Cookbook

Hasty Tasty Chef
© 2018

Easy Bake Oven Cookbook: Easy Peasy Lemon Squeezy
All rights reserved
December 4, 2018
Copyright ©2018 Dess-Varnedore Group, LLC
HastyTastyChef@gmail.com

NOTE TO PARENTS / GUARDIANS:
Adult assistance required for safety and sanitary purposes

Welcome to the Hasty Tasty family! We love having fun with all of the Jr Chef's that join us and we're so glad you're here!

Are you wanting to cook something sweet? How about something savory? It doesn't matter if you want cake, brownies or cookies or maybe even pizza and bread sticks. You can find it all in your new cookbook.

Do you want something you can whip up in a minute? You can surely do this by creating a "semi" homemade cake. You simply start with a cake mix base from a box! Easy Peasy! We've got lots and lots of recipes for you to choose from.

There may also be times you want to make everything from scratch. Honestly, that doesn't happen quiet as much in our kitchen, but on a rare occasion, it does happen. Because we want you to have what you need, your new cookbook also includes several "from scratch" recipes that you can enjoy!

Want to see pictures of the recipes in this book? Join us on the Hasty Tasty Facebook™ page! We'd love to see your pics also!

Can you please do the Hasty Tasty Chef a huge favor? *(because we could sure use your help)*

It would help **_so much_** if you would head over to Amazon and leave a quick review for our book. It only takes a minute, but it helps more than you can ever imagine.

I certainly hope that you find the recipes helpful. We would love to see a picture of your creations! And we've got some we want to share with you!

Find The Hasty Tasty Chef on Facebook and join in on all the fun today!

*Here are a few **Tips For Success** that we hope will help:*

When a recipe calls for **all purpose flour**, we like to use White Lily™ brand for a fluffy and light cake. We also use cake flour if we are out of White Lily. You can use whatever you have access to. We just wanted to share what works for us.

Always preheat your oven before mixing the ingredients for the cake.

Quick Tip: Want to cook more than one cake at a time or test out a recipe? Your EASY-BAKE oven cooks at about 350 degrees F. You can easily set your regular oven to the same temperature and use it to test out your recipes or to cook multiple items at once. Please follow all safety precautions.

Cooking Brownies: Brownies will continue to cook a little even after you pull them out of the oven. They will not look done like your cakes will. Always test your brownies by inserting a clean toothpick into the center and removing to check for uncooked batter on the toothpick. Check frequently to ensure that you do not overcook your brownies.

Table of Contents

Cakes

Vanilla Cake

Ingredients:

- 4 tablespoons all purpose flour

- 2 tablespoons sugar

- ½ teaspoon baking powder

- Small pinch of salt

- 4 tablespoons milk

- ¼ teaspoon vanilla extract

- 2 tablespoons butter (softened)

Directions:

Preheat oven. Spray pans with nonstick spray

1. Mix all dry ingredients together in small bowl. Set aside

2. Cream together butter, milk and vanilla

3. Slowly add in dry ingredients

4. Pour batter into ban to fill ½ full. Bake approximately 10 minutes

5. Remove and allow to cool

6. Top with frosting of your choice

Chocolate Cake *(from scratch)*

Ingredients:

- 4 tablespoons all purpose flour

- 2 tablespoons sugar

- ½ teaspoon baking powder

- Small pinch of salt

- 2 teaspoons unsweetened cocoa

- 4 tablespoons milk

- 2 tablespoons butter (softened)

Directions:

1. Preheat oven. Spray pans with nonstick spray

2. Mix all dry ingredients together in small bowl. Set aside

3. Cream together butter, milk and vanilla

4. Slowly add in dry ingredients

5. Pour batter into ban to fill ½ full. Bake approximately 10 minutes

6. Remove and allow to cool

7. Top with frosting of your choice

Sprinkles Cake *(from scratch)*

Ingredients:

- 4 tablespoons all purpose flour

- 2 tablespoons granulated sugar

- ½ teaspoon baking powder

- Small pinch salt

- 4 tablespoons milk

- ¼ teaspoon vanilla extract

- 2 tablespoons butter (softened)

- ½ tablespoon sprinkles

Directions:

1. Preheat oven. Spray pans with nonstick spray

2. Mix all dry ingredients together in small bowl. Set aside (except for sprinkles

3. Cream together butter, milk and vanilla

4. Slowly add in dry ingredients until well blended

5. Gently fold in sprinkles

6. Pour batter into ban to fill ½ full. Bake approximately 10 minutes

7. Remove and allow to cool. Top with frosting of choice

Easy Vanilla Cake *(box mix)*

Ingredients:

- 4 tablespoons vanilla cake box mix

- 2 tablespoons milk

- 1 tablespoon applesauce or egg

- 1 teaspoon butter (softened)

Directions:

1. Preheat oven. Spray pans with nonstick spray

2. Mix all ingredients together in small bowl

3. Fill pan ½ - ¾ full with cake batter

4. Place pan into the oven and cook for 8–10 minutes

5. Remove cake from oven and allow it to cool

6. Top with frosting of your choice

Easy White Cake *(box mix)*

Ingredients:

- 4 tablespoons white cake box mix

- 2 tablespoons milk

- 1 tablespoon applesauce or egg

- 1 teaspoon butter (softened)

Directions:

1. Preheat oven. Spray pans with nonstick spray

2. Mix all ingredients together in small bowl

3. Fill pan ½ - ¾ full with cake batter

4. Place pan into the oven and cook for 8-10 minutes

5. Remove cake from oven and allow it to cool

6. Top with frosting of your choice

Yummy Chocolate Cake *(box mix)*

Ingredients:

- 4 tablespoons chocolate cake box mix

- 2 tablespoons HOT water

- 1 tablespoon applesauce or egg

- 1 teaspoon butter (softened)

Directions:

1. Preheat oven. Spray pans with nonstick spray

2. Mix all ingredients together in small bowl

3. Fill pan ½ - ¾ full with cake batter

4. Place pan into the oven and cook for 8-10 minutes

5. Remove cake from oven and allow it to cool

6. Top with frosting of your choice

Super Strawberry Cake *(box mix)*

Ingredients:

- 4 tablespoons strawberry cake box mix

- 2 tablespoons milk

- 1 tablespoon applesauce or egg

- 1 teaspoon butter (softened)

Directions:

1. Preheat oven. Spray pans with nonstick spray

2. Mix all ingredients together in small bowl

3. Fill pan ½ - ¾ full with cake batter

4. Place pan into the oven and cook for 8-10 minutes

5. Remove cake from oven and allow it to cool

6. Top with frosting of your choice

Rainbow Cake *(box mix)*

Ingredients:

- 4 tablespoons white cake box mix

- 2 tablespoons milk

- 1 tablespoon applesauce or egg

- 1 teaspoon butter (softened)

- Food coloring of your choice

Directions:

1. Preheat oven. Spray pans with nonstick spray

2. Mix all ingredients together in small bowl

3. Divide batter into separate bowls (one bowl for each food color that you will be using)

4. Add food coloring to each bowl and mix to achieve desired color

5. Drop spoonfuls of colored batter into greased pan in whatever design pattern you like. Do not fill pan more that halfway full to the top.

6. Place pan into the oven and cook for 8-10 minutes

7. Remove cake from oven and allow it to cool

8. Top with frosting of your choice. Sprinkle with colored sugar for an extra pop of color!

Orange Soda Pop Cake *(box mix)*

Ingredients:

- 4 tablespoons white cake box mix

- 3 tablespoons orange flavored carbonated soda pop

Directions:

1. Preheat oven. Spray pan with nonstick spray

2. Mix all ingredients together in small bowl

3. Fill pan ¾ full with batter

4. Bake 12–14 minutes

5. Remove pan from oven and allow to cool

6. Top with frosting of your choice. Sprinkle with colored sugar for an extra pop of color!

Root Beer Soda Pop Cake *(box mix)*

Ingredients:

- 4 tablespoons white cake box mix

- 3 tablespoons root beer flavored carbonated soda pop

Directions:

1. Preheat oven. Spray pan with nonstick spray

2. Mix all ingredients together in small bowl

3. Fill pan ¾ full with batter

4. Bake 12-14 minutes

5. Remove pan from oven and allow to cool

6. Top with frosting of your choice. Sprinkle with colored sugar for an extra pop of color!

Cookies & Creme Cake *(box mix)*

Cake Ingredients:

- 6 tablespoons chocolate cake box mix

- 3 tablespoons HOT water

- 1 ½ tablespoon applesauce or egg

- 1 ½ teaspoon butter (softened)

Topping:

- ½ - ¾ cup non dairy whipped topping

- 4 crushed Oreo cookies

- Chocolate syrup (optional)

Directions:

1. Preheat oven. Spray pans with nonstick spray

2. Mix all ingredients together in small bowl

3. Fill pan ½ - ¾ full with cake batter

4. Place pan into the oven and cook for 8-10 minutes

5. Remove cake from oven and cook the second cake

6. Allow both cakes to cool completely before topping

7. Spread ½ of the whipped topping on 1st cake and then sprinkle ½ of the crushed Oreo cookies on top of whipped topping

8. Place 2nd cake on top of crushed cookies and layer with remaining whipped topping and crushed cookies. Drizzle with chocolate syrup if desired.

2 Layer Strawberry JellO Cake *(box mix)*

Ingredients:

- 1/3 cup vanilla cake box mix

- 1 tablespoon milk

- 1 tablespoon strawberry Jello

- 2 teaspoons oil

- 1 egg white

Ingredients (Topping):

- ½ cup thawed whipped topping (ex: Coolwhip)

- 2 tablespoons powdered sugar

- ½ tsp strawberry Jello mix

Cake Directions:

1. Preheat oven. Spray pans with nonstick spray

2. Mix all ingredients together in small bowl

3. Divide batter into 2 pans

4. Place pan into the oven and cook for 8–10 minutes or until sides start to pull away from pan

5. Remove cake from oven and allow it to cool

Icing Directions:

6. Top cake #1 with ½ of the whipped topping.
7. Place powdered sugar and ½ teaspoon of strawberry jello into a plastic bag.

8. Add a few drops of water and kneed the bag until ingredients are mixed and form a glaze.

9. Cut a very small portion of the corner off of the bag to make an opening for the glaze to come out of

10. Drizzle ½ of the glaze over the whipped topping on the first cake

11. Add the second cake on top of 1st cake and repeat layering the remaining whipped topping and glaze over the top of the second cake.

Strawberry Soda Pop Cake *(box mix)*

Ingredients:

- 4 tablespoons white cake box mix

- 3 tablespoons strawberry flavored carbonated soda pop

Directions:

1. Preheat oven. Spray pan with nonstick spray

2. Mix all ingredients together in small bowl

3. Fill pan ¾ full with batter

4. Bake 12-14 minutes

5. Remove pan from oven and allow to cool

6. Top with frosting of your choice. Sprinkle with colored sugar for an extra pop of color!

Cream Soda Pop Cake *(box mix)*

Ingredients:

- 4 tablespoons white cake box mix

- 3 tablespoons cream soda flavored carbonated soda pop

Directions:

1. Preheat oven. Spray pan with nonstick spray

2. Mix all ingredients together in small bowl

3. Fill pan ¾ full with batter

4. Bake 12–14 minutes

5. Remove pan from oven and allow to cool

6. Top with frosting of your choice. Sprinkle with colored sugar for an extra pop of color!

Basic Soda Pop Cake *(box mix)*

Ingredients:

- 4 tablespoons white cake box mix

- 3 tablespoons of your favorite carbonated beverage

Directions:

1. Preheat oven. Spray pan with nonstick spray

2. Mix all ingredients together in small bowl

3. Fill pan ¾ full with batter

4. Bake 12-14 minutes

5. Remove pan from oven and allow to cool

6. Top with frosting of your choice. Sprinkle with colored sugar for an extra pop of color!

Peanut Butter & Chocolate Cake *(box mix)*

Ingredients:

- 4 tablespoons yellow cake box mix

- 2 tablespoons milk

- ½ tablespoon applesauce

- 1 tablespoon peanut butter.

- Chocolate icing

Directions:

1. Preheat oven. Spray pan with nonstick spray

2. Mix all ingredients together in small bowl except for chocolate icing

3. Fill pan ¾ full with batter

4. Bake 12-14 minutes until cake pulls away from sides

5. Remove pan from oven and allow to cool

6. Top with chocolate icing

Lemonade Cake *(box mix)*

Ingredients:

- 4 tablespoons yellow cake box mix

- 2 tablespoons milk

- 1 tablespoon applesauce

- 1 teaspoon butter (softened).

- 1 packet individual lemonade drink mix (the kind that you normally mix in a bottle of water)

Directions:

1. Preheat oven. Spray pan with nonstick spray

2. Mix all ingredients together in small bowl

3. Fill pan ¾ full with batter

4. Bake 10 minutes or until cake pulls away from sides

5. Remove pan from oven and allow to cool

6. Top with icing of choice

Note: I love this cake but it is very lemony! Cut the lemonade mix down if you want a little less "lemon" flavor. This cake goes great with cream cheese icing

Peanut Butter & Jelly Cake *(box mix)*

Ingredients (cake):

- 4 tablespoons yellow cake box mix

- 2 tablespoons milk

- ½ tablespoon applesauce

- 1 tablespoon peanut butter.

Icing:

- 4 tablespoons Jelly of choice

- 1 ½ tablespoon sugar

Directions:

1. Preheat oven. Spray pan with nonstick spray

2. Mix all cake ingredients together in small bowl

3. Fill pan ¾ full with batter

4. Bake 12-14 minutes until cake pulls away from sides

5. Remove pan from oven and allow to cool

6. Mix jelly and sugar together and use as icing on the cake

Apple Jelly Cake *(box mix)*

Ingredients:

- 4 tablespoons vanilla cake box mix

- 2 tablespoons milk

- 1 tablespoon applesauce or egg

- 1 teaspoon butter (softened)

Icing:

- 4 tablespoons apple jelly

- 1 ½ tablespoon sugar

Directions:

1. Preheat oven. Spray pans with nonstick spray

2. Mix all cake ingredients together in small bowl

3. Fill pan ¾ full with batter

4. Place pan into the oven and cook for 8-10 minutes

5. Remove cake from oven and allow it to cool

6. Mix together apple jelly and sugar and use as the icing on the cake

Pineapple Upside Down Cake *(box mix)*

Ingredients:

- 4 tablespoons yellow cake box mix

- 2 tablespoons milk

- 1 ½ tablespoon egg (beaten)

- 1 teaspoon butter (softened).

- 3 tablespoons crushed pineapple

- 1 ½ tablespoons firmly packed brown sugar

- 3-4 Maraschino cherry (optional)

Directions:

1. Preheat oven. Spray pan with nonstick spray

2. Mix pineapple and brown sugar together in small bowl. Add chopped cherry's if desired

3. Spoon into bottom of cake pan

4. Mix remaining ingredients together in small bowl

5. Fill pan ¾ full with batter

6. Bake 10-12 minutes or until cake pulls away from sides

7. Remove pan from oven and allow to cool

Fun Birthday Cake *(box mix)*

Ingredients:

- 4 tablespoons funfetti cake box mix

- 2 tablespoons milk

- 1 tablespoon applesauce or egg

- 1 teaspoon butter (softened)

- Sprinkles

Directions:

1. Preheat oven. Spray pans with nonstick spray

2. Mix all ingredients (except for sprinkles) together in small bowl

3. Fill pan ¾ full with mixed batter

4. Place pan into the oven and cook for approximately 10 minutes

5. Remove cake from oven and allow it to cool

6. Use frosting of your choice and top with sprinkles

Red Velvet Cake *(box mix)*

Ingredients (cake):

- 4 tablespoons red velvet cake box mix

- 2 tablespoons HOT water

- 1 tablespoon applesauce or egg

- 1 teaspoon butter (softened)

- 2 tablespoons chopped pecans (optional)

Icing:
- Cream cheese icing (see icing recipes or use ready made)

Directions:
1. Preheat oven. Spray pans with nonstick spray

2. Mix all cake ingredients together in small bowl

3. Fill pan ¾ full with mixed batter

4. Place pan into the oven and cook for approximately 10 minutes

5. Remove cake from oven and allow it to cool

6. Top with delicious cream cheese icing
7. Optional: Sprinkle top of cake with chopped pecans

Carrot Cake *(box mix)*

Ingredients (cake):

- 4 tablespoons carrot cake box mix

- 2 tablespoons milk

- 1 tablespoon applesauce or egg

- 1 teaspoon butter (softened)

- 1 teaspoon raisens (optional)

- 1 tablespoon chopped pecans (optional)

Icing:
- Cream cheese icing (see icing recipes or use ready made)

Directions:
1. Preheat oven. Spray pans with nonstick spray

2. Mix all cake ingredients together in small bowl

3. Fill pan ¾ full with mixed batter

4. Place pan into the oven and cook for approximately 10 minutes

5. Remove cake from oven and allow it to cool

6. Top with delicious cream cheese icing

Red Velvet and Chocolate Chip Cake *(box mix)*

Ingredients (cake):

- 4 tablespoons red velvet cake box mix

- 2 tablespoons HOT water

- 1 tablespoon applesauce or egg

- 1 teaspoon butter (softened)

- 1 ½ teaspoons white chocolate chips

Directions:

1. Preheat oven. Spray pans with nonstick spray

2. Mix all ingredients together in small bowl

3. Fill pan ¾ full with mixed batter

4. Place pan into the oven and cook for approximately 10-12 minutes or until cake pulls away from side of pan slightly

5. Remove cake from oven and allow it to cool

6. Top with Glaze icing (see icing recipes)

Pineapple Angel Food Cake *(box mix)*

Ingredients (cake):

- 4 tablespoons white angel food cake box mix

- 5 tablespoons crushed pineapple with juice

Ingredients (icing):

- 1 tablespoon instant vanilla pudding mix

- 5 tablespoons crushed pineapple with juice

- 2 tablespoons thawed whipped topping

Directions:

1. Preheat oven. Spray pan with nonstick spray

2. Mix all cake ingredients together in small bowl

3. Fill pan ½ - ¾ full with batter

4. Bake 12-15 minutes or until cake pulls away from sides

5. Remove pan from oven and allow to cool

Icing:

6. Mix instant vanilla pudding and pineapple (with juice) together in bowl. Fold in whipped topping

7. Apply to top of cooled cake

Red Velvet Ice Cream Sandwich *(box mix)*

Ingredients (cake):

- 6 tablespoons red velvet cake box mix

- 3 tablespoons HOT water

- 1 ½ tablespoons applesauce or egg (beaten)

- 1 ½ teaspoon butter (softened)

- ¼ teaspoon vanilla extract

Center Filling

- ½ – ¾ cup vanilla ice cream (softened)

Directions:
1. Preheat oven. Spray pan with nonstick spray
2. Mix all cake ingredients together in small bowl
3. Divide batter into two pans
4. Bake each pan 10-12 minutes or until cake pulls away from sides
5. Remove pan from oven and allow to cool completely
6. Spread ice cream over top of cake #1. Layer cake #2 on top to form an ice cream sandwich cake
7. Place in freezer until the ice cream is frozen.
8. Slice into bars and serve immediately

Chocolate Ice Cream Sandwich *(box mix)*

Ingredients (cake):

- 6 tablespoons chocolate cake box mix

- 3 tablespoons HOT water

- 1 ½ tablespoons egg (beaten)

- 1 ½ teaspoon butter (softened)

- ¼ teaspoon vanilla extract

Center Filling

- ½ – ¾ cup vanilla ice cream (softened)

Directions:

1. Preheat oven. Spray pan with nonstick spray

2. Mix all cake ingredients together in small bowl

3. Divide batter into two pans

4. Bake each pan 10-12 minutes or until cake pulls away from sides

5. Remove pan from oven and allow cake to cool completely

6. Spread ice cream over top of cake #1. Layer cake #2 on top to form an ice cream sandwich cake

7. Place in freezer until the ice cream is frozen.

8. Slice into bars and serve immediately

Strawberry Ice Cream Sandwich *(box mix)*

Ingredients (cake):

- 6 tablespoons strawberry cake box mix

- 3 tablespoons milk

- 1 ½ tablespoons egg (beaten)

- 1 ½ teaspoon butter (softened)

- ¼ teaspoon vanilla extract

Center Filling

- ½ – ¾ cup vanilla ice cream (softened)

Directions:

1. Preheat oven. Spray pan with nonstick spray

2. Mix all cake ingredients together in small bowl

3. Divide batter into two pans

4. Bake each pan 10-12 minutes or until cake pulls away from sides

5. Remove pan from oven and allow cake to cool completely

6. Spread ice cream over top of cake #1. Layer cake #2 on top to form an ice cream sandwich cake

7. Place in freezer until the ice cream is frozen.

8. Slice into bars and serve immediately

Peanut Butter Cup Ice Cream Sandwich

Ingredients (cake):

- 6 tablespoons yellow cake box mix

- 3 tablespoons milk

- tablespoons egg (beaten)

- 1 ½ teaspoon Peanut butter

- ¼ teaspoon vanilla extract

Center Filling

- ½ – ¾ cup chocolate ice cream (softened)

Directions:

1. Preheat oven. Spray pan with nonstick spray

2. Mix all cake ingredients together in small bowl

3. Divide batter into two pans

4. Bake each pan 10-12 minutes or until cake pulls away from sides

5. Remove pan from oven and allow cake to cool completely

6. Spread ice cream over top of cake #1. Layer cake #2 on top to form an ice cream sandwich cake

7. Place in freezer until the ice cream is frozen.

8. Slice into bars and serve immediately

Mug Mix Recipes for Easy Bake Ovens

Can I let you in on a secret shortcut to great Easy Bake Oven cakes? Shhhhh.... Don't tell anyone. Ready made mug mixes. Yes, I'm talking about the ones you find in the cake aisle of your grocery store or at the click of a mouse online. Easy Peasy.

I've tried both Duncan Hines™ Perfect Size for 1 and Betty Crocker™ Mug treats and I love them both.

Basic Vanilla Bean Cake *(from mug mix)*

Ingredients:

- 1 Packet Vanilla Bean Mug Mix

- 3 tablespoons milk or water

- 1/8 teaspoon vanilla extract (optional)

Directions:

1. Preheat oven. Spray pans with nonstick spray

2. Mix all ingredients together in small bowl

3. Fill pan ½ - ¾ full with mixed batter

4. Place pan into the oven and cook for approximately 10 – 12 minutes

5. Remove cake from oven and allow it to cool

6. Top with icing of your choice

Orange Vanilla Bean Cake *(from mug mix)*

Ingredients:

- 1 Packet Vanilla Bean Mug Mix

- 3 tablespoons milk or water

- 1/8 teaspoon orange extract

Directions:

1. Preheat oven. Spray pans with nonstick spray

2. Mix all ingredients together in small bowl

3. Fill pan ½ - ¾ full with mixed batter

4. Place pan into the oven and cook for approximately 10 – 12 minutes

5. Remove cake from oven and allow it to cool

6. Top with vanilla icing

Lemon Cake *(from mug mix)*

Ingredients:

- 1 Packet lemon cake Mug Mix

- 3 tablespoons milk or water

- 1/8 teaspoon vanilla extract (optional)

Directions:

1. Preheat oven. Spray pans with nonstick spray

2. Mix all ingredients together in small bowl

3. Fill pan ½ – ¾ full with mixed batter

4. Place pan into the oven and cook for approximately 10 – 12 minutes

5. Remove cake from oven and allow it to cool

6. Top with lemon glaze or icing of choice

Chocolate Brownie *(from mug mix)*

Ingredients:

- 1 Packet Chocolate Brownie Mug Mix

- 3 tablespoons HOT water

- 1/8 teaspoon vanilla extract (optional)

Directions:

1. Preheat oven. Spray pans with nonstick spray

2. Mix all ingredients together in small bowl

3. Fill pan ½ – ¾ full with mixed batter

4. Place pan into the oven and cook for approximately 10 – 12 minutes

5. Remove cake from oven and allow it to cool

6. Top with vanilla ice cream and chocolate syrup if desired. Can also top with thawed whipped topping and add chocolate sprinkles. Yum!!

Moist Chocolate Cake *(from mug mix)*

Ingredients:

- 1 Packet Chocolate Cake Mug Mix

- 3 tablespoons HOT water

- ½ teaspoon chocolate chips (optional)

- 1/8 teaspoon vanilla extract (optional)

Directions:

1. Preheat oven. Spray pans with nonstick spray

2. Mix all ingredients together in small bowl

3. Fill pan ½ - ¾ full with mixed batter

4. Place pan into the oven and cook for approximately 10 – 12 minutes

5. Remove cake from oven and allow it to cool

6. Top with icing of choice or thawed whipped topping

White Chocolate Chip Cake *(from mug mix)*

Ingredients:

- 1 Packet Chocolate Cake Mug Mix

- 3 tablespoons HOT water

- ½ – ¾ teaspoon white chocolate chips

- 1/8 teaspoon vanilla extract (optional)

Icing:

- ½ cup thawed whipped topping

- Chocolate syrup or glaze *(*see chocolate glaze recipe in Icing recipes)*

Directions:

1. Preheat oven. Spray pans with nonstick spray

2. Mix all ingredients together in small bowl

3. Fill pan ½ – ¾ full with mixed batter

4. Place pan into the oven and cook for approximately 10 – 12 minutes

5. Remove cake from oven and allow it to cool

6. Top with thawed whipped topping and drizzle chocolate syrup or glaze over cake.

Chocolate Chip Cookie Cake *(from mug mix)*

Ingredients:

- 1 Packet Chocolate Chip Cookie Cake Mug Mix

- 1 tablespoon plus 1 teaspoon milk

- 1/8 teaspoon vanilla extract (optional)

Icing:

- Chocolate syrup or chocolate glaze (from icing recipes)

Directions:

1. Preheat oven. Spray pans with nonstick spray

2. Mix all ingredients together in small bowl

3. Fill pan ½ - ¾ full with mixed batter

4. Place pan into the oven and cook for **approximately 10 – 12** minutes

5. Remove cake from oven

6. Drizzle chocolate syrup or glaze over top

7. Serve immediately

Cookies and Cream Cake (from mug mix)

Ingredients:

- 1 Packet Cookies & Cream Cake Mug Mix

- 3 tablespoons milk

- 1/8 teaspoon vanilla extract (optional)

Icing:

- ¼ – ½ cup Thawed whipped topping

- 2-4 crushed Oreo cookies

Directions:

1. Preheat oven. Spray pans with nonstick spray

2. Mix all ingredients together in small bowl

3. Fill pan ½ – ¾ full with mixed batter

4. Place pan into the oven and cook for approximately 10 – 12 minutes

5. Remove cake from oven and allow to cool completely

6. Top cake with thawed whipped topping

7. Sprinkle crushed Oreo's on top of cake

S'mores Cake (from mug mix)

Ingredients:

- 1 Packet S'mores Cake Mug Mix

- 3 tablespoons milk

- 1/8 teaspoon vanilla extract (optional)

Icing:

- Chocolate syrup or chocolate glaze (from icing recipes)

- 2 graham crackers crushed (optional)

Directions:

1. Preheat oven. Spray pans with nonstick spray

2. Mix all ingredients together in small bowl

3. Fill pan ½ - ¾ full with mixed batter

4. Place pan into the oven and cook for approximately 10 – 12 minutes

5. Remove cake from oven

6. Drizzle chocolate syrup or glaze over top. Can also sprinkle crushed graham crackers over cake if desired.

7. Serve immediately

Strawberry Shortcake *(from mug mix)*

Ingredients:

- 1 Packet Strawberry Shortcake Mug Mix

- 3 tablespoons milk

- 1/8 teaspoon vanilla extract (optional)

Icing:

- ¼ – ½ cup Thawed whipped topping (optional)

- ½ teaspoon colored sugar (optional)

Directions:

1. Preheat oven. Spray pans with nonstick spray

2. Mix all ingredients together in small bowl

3. Fill pan ½ – ¾ full with mixed batter

4. Place pan into the oven and cook for approximately 10 – 12 minutes

5. Remove cake from oven

6. Sprinkle colored sugar on top (optional)

7. Top cake with thawed whipped topping if desired

Blueberry Muffin Cake *(from mug mix)*

Ingredients:

- 1 Packet Blueberry Muffin Cake Mug Mix

- 3 tablespoons milk

- 1/8 teaspoon vanilla extract (optional)

Icing:

¼ - ½ cup Thawed whipped topping (optional)
Or Vanilla glaze

Directions:

1. Preheat oven. Spray pans with nonstick spray

2. Mix all ingredients together in small bowl

3. Fill pan ½ - ¾ full with mixed batter

4. Place pan into the oven and cook for approximately 10 – 12 minutes

5. Remove cake from oven

6. Top cake with thawed whipped topping if desired. Can also top with a vanilla glaze (see recipe in Icing recipe chapter)

Cinnamon Roll Cake *(from mug mix)*

Ingredients:

- 1 Packet Cinnamon Roll Mug Mix

- 3 tablespoons milk

- 1/8 teaspoon vanilla extract (optional)

Icing:

- glaze

Directions:

1. Preheat oven. Spray pans with nonstick spray

2. Mix all ingredients together in small bowl

3. Fill pan ½ – ¾ full with mixed batter

4. Place pan into the oven and cook for approximately 10 – 12 minutes

5. Remove cake from oven

6. Immediately top cake with glaze

Chocolate Peanut Butter Cake *(from mug mix)*

Ingredients:

- 1 Packet Chocolate Cake Mug Mix
- 3 tablespoons HOT water
- 1/8 teaspoon vanilla extract (optional)

Icing:

- Peanut Butter Icing (see recipe in Icing section)
- 1 teaspoon chocolate chips (optional)

Directions:

1. Preheat oven. Spray pans with nonstick spray
2. Mix all cake ingredients together in small bowl
3. Fill pan ½ - ¾ full with mixed batter
4. Place pan into the oven and cook for approximately 10 – 12 minutes
5. Remove cake from oven and allow to cool
6. Top with Peanut Butter icing
7. Sprinkle chocolate chips over top (optional)

Cookies

Chocolate Cookies *(from mug mix)*

Ingredients:

- 1 Packet Chocolate Cake Mug Mix

- 1 tablespoon milk

Directions:

1. Preheat oven. Spray pans with nonstick spray

2. Mix ingredients together in small bowl

3. Roll cookie mixture into ½ to ¾ inch balls

4. Place on pan and flatten into cookie shape

5. Place pan into the oven and cook for approximately 9–11 minutes

6. Remove cookies from oven and cool

Chocolate Chip Cookies *(from box cake mix)*

Ingredients:

4 tablespoons yellow cake mix

1 tablespoon egg (beaten) or applesauce

½ teaspoon vanilla extract

¾ tablespoon butter (softened)

4 tablespoons semi- sweet chocolate chips

Directions:

1. Preheat oven. Spray pans with nonstick spray

2. Mix ingredients together in small bowl

3. Roll cookie mixture into ½ to ¾ inch balls

4. Place on pan and flatten into cookie shape

5. Place pan into the oven and cook for approximately 9–11 minutes

6. Remove cookies from oven and cool

Yummy Cookie Butter Cookies (from scratch)

Ingredients:

- 3 tablespoons all purpose flour

- 1 tablespoon egg (beaten) or applesauce

- 1 tablespoon brown sugar

- 1 tablespoon butter (melted)

- 1 tablespoons semi- sweet chocolate chips

- 1 tablespoon Nutella™

Directions:

1. Preheat oven. Spray pans with nonstick spray

2. Mix ingredients together in small bowl

3. Drop mixture by spoonful onto pan

4. Place pan into the oven and cook for approximately 9–11 minutes

5. Remove cookies from oven and cool

Peanut Butter Cookie Cups *(from cookie dough)*

Ingredients:

- 1 package refrigerated peanut butter cookie dough

- Hershey's kisses

Directions:

1. Preheat oven. Spray pans with nonstick spray

2. Roll cookie mixture into ½ to ¾ inch balls

3. Place on pan and flatten into cookie shape

4. Place pan into the oven and cook for approximately 9–11 minutes

5. Unwrap 1 Hershey's kiss for each cookie

6. Remove cookies from oven

7. Place one Hershey's kiss on top of each cookie and press down into cookie as the chocolate begins to melt

Chocolate Peanut Butter Cookies *(from box mix)*

Ingredients:

- 4 tablespoons chocolate fudge cake mix

- 1 ½ tablespoon eggs (beaten) or applesauce

- 1/8 teaspoon vanilla extract

- 1 ½ tablespoons peanut butter

- 3 tablespoons semi- sweet chocolate chips

- ½ tablespoon water

Directions:
1. Preheat oven. Spray pans with nonstick spray

2. Mix ingredients together in small bowl

3. Roll cookie mixture into ½ to ¾ inch balls

4. Place on pan and flatten into cookie shape

5. Place pan into the oven and cook for approximately 9–11 minutes

6. Remove cookies from oven and cool

7. Frost with icing of choice or thawed whipped topping if desired

Lady Finger Cookies *(from scratch)*

Ingredients:

- 4 tablespoons all purpose flour

- 1 tablespoon powdered sugar

- 2 tablespoons butter (softened)

- 1/8 teaspoon vanilla extract

- 2 tablespoons chopped pecans or walnuts

- Additional powdered sugar to roll warm cookies in

Directions:

1. Preheat oven. Spray pans with nonstick spray

2. Mix cookie ingredients together in small bowl

3. Roll cookie mixture into desired shape

4. Roll cookie in additional powdered sugar

5. Place on pan and flatten into cookie shape

6. Place pan into the oven and cook for approximately 9-11 minutes

7. Remove cookies from oven and immediately roll in powdered sugar again to coat the cookies

Birthday Cake Cookies *(from box mix)*

Ingredients:

- 4 tablespoons funfetti cake mix

- 1 tablespoon egg (beaten) or applesauce

- ½ teaspoon vanilla extract

- ½ tablespoon butter (softened)

- 1/8 teaspoon baking powder

- 1/8 teaspoon vanilla extract

- 2 tablespoons sprinkles

Directions:

1. Preheat oven. Spray pans with nonstick spray

2. Mix ingredients together in small bowl

3. Roll cookie mixture into 1 inch balls

4. Place on pan and flatten into cookie shape

5. Place pan into the oven and cook for approximately 9–11 minutes

6. Remove cookies from oven and cool

7. Top with frosting & sprinkles for that true birthday cake feel!

Cake Batter Peanut Butter Cookies *(from box mix)*

Ingredients:

- 4 tablespoons yellow cake mix
- 2 tablespoon egg (beaten) or applesauce
- ½ tablespoon brown sugar
- 2 tablespoons peanut butter
- 1 teaspoon water
- ½ tablespoon oil

Topping:

- Sugar

Directions:

1. Preheat oven. Spray pans with nonstick spray
2. Mix ingredients together in small bowl
3. Roll cookie mixture into 1 inch balls
4. Roll cookies in granulated sugar to coat
5. Place on pan and flatten into cookie shape
6. Place pan into the oven and cook for approximately 9 minutes
7. Remove cookies from oven and cool

Basic Sandwich Cookies (from refrigerated dough)

Ingredients (cookies):

- Any flavor refrigerated cookie dough
- All purpose flour (optional)

Filling:

- Your choice of assorted frostings, ice cream or peanut butter
- Sprinkles or assorted candies (ex. M&M's ™)

Directions:

1. Preheat oven. Spray pans with nonstick spray
2. Remove desired amount of cookie dough from wrapper (depending on how many cookies you want to make). Refrigerate remaining dough
3. Roll dough to ¼ inch thickness. You can sprinkle a little flour down first to keep the cookies from sticking if you'd like.
4. Cut out cookies using a small round cookie cutter
5. Place cookies on sheet making sure to leave enough room between them (1-2 inches)
6. Bake until edges are just slightly brown (usually 8-10 minutes)
7. Remove and allow cookies to cool completely
8. Spread desired filling on the underside of the 1st cookie. Top with the second cookie and press together
9. Roll cookie edges in sprinkles or assorted candies

Cake Batter Cookies (from box mix)

Ingredients (cookies):

- 4 tablespoons white cake mix
- 4 tablespoons Betty Crocker ™ sugar cookie mix from pouch
- 1 tablespoon butter (melted)
- 1 ½ tablespoons applesauce or beaten egg
- 1/8 teaspoon vanilla extract
- ½ tablespoon sprinkles

Icing:

- 1 tablespoon butter (softened)
- 6 tablespoons powdered sugar
- 1 – 1 ½ teaspoons milk
- 1/8 teaspoon vanilla extract
- Sprinkles

Directions:

1. Preheat oven. Spray pans with nonstick spray
2. Mix all cookie ingredients together well
3. Roll cookies into balls and place on pan
4. Flatten cookies below the top level of the pan
5. Cook for approximately 10 minutes
6. Remove from oven and top with sprinkles

Chocolate Peanut Butter Sandwich Cookies

Ingredients (cookies):

- 4 tablespoons yellow cake mix

- 2 tablespoon egg (beaten) or applesauce

- ½ tablespoon brown sugar

- 2 tablespoons peanut butter

- 1 teaspoon water

- ½ tablespoon oil

Topping:

- Sugar

- Chocolate frosting

Directions:

1. Preheat oven. Spray pans with nonstick spray

2. Mix cookie ingredients together in small bowl

3. Roll cookie mixture into 1 inch balls

4. Roll cookies in granulated sugar to coat

5. Place on pan and flatten into cookie shape

6. Place pan into the oven and cook for approximately 8–10 minutes

7. Remove cookies from oven and cool

8. Spread chocolate frosting of choice on bottom of two cookies and press together to form the chocolate peanut butter sandwich

Fruity Fingers (from refrigerated cookie dough)

Ingredients (cookies):

- Refrigerated sugar cookie dough
- ½ cup crushed Fruit flavored cereal (divided)

Directions:

1. Remove desired amount of cookie dough from wrapper (depending on how many cookies you want to make). Refrigerate remaining dough
2. Mix together 1 teaspoon crushed cereal and cookie dough
3. Roll dough into balls and refrigerate for 1 hour
4. Preheat oven and spray pans with nonstick spray
5. Roll cookie balls into 2-3 inch long "fingers" (ropes)
6. Coat cookies by rolling in cereal
7. Place cookies on sheet making sure to leave enough room between them (1-2 inches)
8. Bake until just slightly brown (usually 8-10 minutes)
9. Remove and allow cookies to cool completely

Tip: I used the spatula to gently "shape" cookies while still warm

Strawberry Cups (from refrigerated cookie dough)

Ingredients (cookies):
- Refrigerated sugar cookie dough
- All purpose flour (optional)
- 2 tablespoons strawberry preserves (*can choose a different flavor preserves if you prefer)

Directions:
1. Remove about 2-3 ounces of dough from the wrapper
2. Roll dough into ¾ inch balls
3. Using your thumb, press down in the center of each ball to form a deep indention making it look like a small "mini" bowl. Flatten slightly to fit in pan
4. Place cookies in freezer for 20 minutes
5. Preheat oven and spray pans with nonstick spray
6. Bake until edges are just slightly brown (usually 8-10 minutes
7. Remove from oven and press back down in center of cookie with the tip of a spoon to form your "mini" bowl again.
8. Place cookies back in oven and cook for an additional 2-3 minutes. Cookies should be golden brown
9. Remove from oven and cool cookies completely
10. Fill the center of your cookie with strawberry preserves

Peanut Butter & Chocolate Spirals *(cookie dough)*

Ingredients (cookies):

- Refrigerated chocolate cookie dough (1/8 of roll)
- Refrigerated peanut butter cookie dough (1/8 of roll)
- 1 ½ teaspoons semi-sweet chocolate chips
- 1 ½ teaspoons peanut butter flavored chips
- ¼ teaspoon all purpose flour

Directions:

1. Remove cookie dough from wrapper. Refrigerate remaining dough
2. Mix together chocolate cookie dough and peanut butter chips. Set aside
3. Mix together peanut butter cookie dough and flour. Add chocolate chips
4. Place both doughs in refrigerator for 1 hour
5. On a floured surface, roll each dough out into a rectangle about 1/8 to ¼ inch thick. You will have one chocolate and one peanut butter rectangle.
6. Place the peanut butter rectangle on top of the chocolate rectangle. Roll up dough to form a "cookie" roll (similar to a pumpkin roll)
7. Refrigerate for 1 additional hour
8. Preheat oven and spray pans with nonstick spray
9. Remove cookie roll from refrigerator and cut into ¼ to ½ inch slices
10. Place on greased pan and bake 10 -12 minutes until just slightly browned.
11. Remove and allow cookies to cool completely

Tip: Get creative! Mix and match any two flavors of refrigerated cookie dough to make it your own. Instead of chocolate and peanut butter chips, try other mix in's that you really like!

Chocolate Peanut Butter Cups *(cookie dough)*

Ingredients (cookies):
- Refrigerated chocolate cookie dough
- All purpose flour (optional)
- 2 tablespoons peanut butter frosting (recipe in frosting section)

Directions:
1. Remove about 2-3 ounces of dough from the wrapper
2. Roll dough into ¾ inch balls
3. Using your thumb, press down in the center of each ball to form a deep indention making it look like a small "mini" bowl
4. Place cookies in freezer for 20 minutes
5. Preheat oven and spray pans with nonstick spray
6. Bake until edges are just slightly browned (usually 8-10 minutes
7. Remove from oven and press back down in center of cookie with the tip of a spoon to form your "mini" bowl again.
8. Place cookies back in oven and cook for an additional 2-3 minutes. Cookies should be firm and set
9. Remove from oven and cool cookies completely
10. Fill center of your cookie "bowl" with peanut butter frosting

Edible Hands (from refrigerated cookie dough)

Ingredients (cookies):

- Refrigerated sugar cookie dough
- All purpose flour (optional)
- Your choice of frosting and candies/ sprinkles to decorate

Directions:

1. Remove desired amount of dough from the wrapper
2. Grease Pans
3. Flatten cookie dough and cover the entire bottom of pan with it.
4. Place hand on top of cookie dough and press down to make a handprint
5. Carefully trim away excess dough from around handprint using a knife (Adult assistance required for this one)
6. Place pan and cookie into freezer for 15 minutes
7. Preheat Oven
8. Remove handprint from freezer and place in oven
9. Cook approximately 6-9 minutes until edges are golden brown
10. Cool Completely

Decorate hand using frosting and candies. Get creative here. You can use different candies for form a bracelet or a ring. You can also make "fingernails" on your hand by placing the same colored candy on the tip of each finger

Cookie Pops (from refrigerated cookie dough)

Ingredients (cookies):

- Refrigerated cookie dough- any flavor (1/8 of roll)
- All purpose flour (optional)
- Your choice of frosting and candies/ sprinkles to decorate

Also Needed:

- 4 inch lollipop sticks (can usually be found in most big box retailers bakery section or arts & crafts stores)
- Small cookie cutters

Directions:

1. Preheat oven and spray pans with nonstick spray
2. Remove about 1/8 of the dough from the wrapper
3. Roll dough on floured surface to about ¼ inch thick
4. Cut out cookies with small cookie cutters. Place one cookie on the pan near the end (leave enough room for it to expand though).
5. Lay lollipop stick so that end of stick in on top of cookie at least ½ inch. Press down slightly so that lollipop tip is embedded in the cookie
6. Gently turn cookie over so that the stick in now on the bottom
7. Bake until edges are slightly brown (7-9 minutes)
8. Decorate with frosting, candies, etc...

Miscellaneous

Cookie Pizza (from cookie dough)

Ingredients

- Refrigerated cookie dough– any flavor (1/8 of roll)
- All purpose flour (optional)
- 2 tablespoons semisweet chocolate chips
- 1 teaspoon shortening (divided)
- 1 ½ teaspoon white chocolate chips
- Your choice of toppings. Some ideas include gummy bears, assorted candies, nuts, chocolate covered raisins, etc...

Directions:

1. Preheat oven and spray pans with nonstick spray
2. Remove about 1/8 of the dough from the wrapper
3. Flatten dough into bottom of greased pan to form "pizza" crust. Leave room around edges for cookie to expand
4. Bake until cookie has set and has become golden brown (12–15 minutes usually)
5. Cool completely in pan
6. Combine ½ teaspoon of shortening with semisweet chocolate chips in a small microwaveable bowl. Microwave for 15 seconds at 70% power and stir. Microwave an additional 10 seconds and stir if not melted. Continue to do so until chocolate is melted.
7. Spread melted chocolate over the crust
8. Add desired "toppings" to pizza
9. Combine ½ teaspoon of shortening with white chocolate chips in a small microwaveable bowl. Microwave for 15 seconds at 70% power and stir. Microwave an additional 10 seconds and stir if not melted. Continue to do so until chocolate is melted.

10. Using a spoon, drizzle the white chocolate over the toppings

Tip: Use red candies or gummies to resemble pepperoni, chocolate covered nuts or raisins to resemble beef, green and yellow candies to resemble peppers topped with melted white chocolate to resemble melted mozzarella cheese.

Pudding Cups (from refrigerated cookie dough)

Ingredients (cookies):

- Refrigerated cookie dough- any flavor
- 2 tablespoons prepared pudding – any flavor
- Sprinkles or colored sugar (optional)

Directions:
1. Remove about 2-3 ounces of dough from the wrapper
2. Roll dough into 1 inch balls and flatten
3. Using your thumb, press down in the center of each ball to form a deep indention making it look like a "mini" bowl
4. Place cookies in freezer for 20 minutes
5. Preheat oven and spray pans with nonstick spray
6. Bake until edges are just slightly brown (usually 8-10 minutes
7. Remove from oven and press back down in center of cookie with the tip of a spoon to form your "mini" bowl again.
8. Place cookies back in oven and cook for an additional 2-3 minutes. Cookies should be golden brown
9. Remove from oven and cool cookies completely
10. Fill the center of your cookie "bowl" with pudding and top with sprinkles or sugar if desired

Cheesecake (from refrigerated cookie dough)

Ingredients:
- Refrigerated sugar cookie dough

Cream Cheese Filling:
- 2 tablespoons cream cheese (softened)
- 2 teaspoons powdered sugar

Topping:
- Fruit, glaze or pie filling (optional)

Directions:

1. Preheat oven and spray pan with nonstick spray
2. Remove enough cookie dough from wrapper to cover the bottom of the pan
3. Press cookie dough evenly onto bottom of pan
4. Bake until golden brown (12–17 minutes usually)
5. Remove from oven and cool
6. Mix together cream cheese and powdered sugar
7. Spread over cooled cookie
8. Top with fruit, pie filling or drizzle a glaze over (optional)

Strawberry Biscuits

Ingredients (biscuits):
- 4 tablespoons Bisquick ™
- 1 ½ teaspoon butter (softened)
- ¾ teaspoon sugar
- 4 teaspoons milk
- 2 teaspoons strawberry preserves

Glaze:
- 2 tablespoons powdered sugar
- 1 teaspoon milk
- 1/8 teaspoon vanilla extract

Directions:
1. Preheat oven and spray pan with nonstick spray
2. Mix Bisquick™, butter and sugar together (mix will be crumbly when ready)
3. Slowly add in milk to form a soft dough
4. Using a ½ teaspoon, drop mix onto pan
5. Form a mini biscuit bowl by pressing your thumb down in center of biscuit leaving indention
6. Fill center indention with strawberry preserves
7. Cook until golden brown (10-14 minutes usually)
8. Combine glaze ingredients and drizzle over warm biscuits

French Toast

Ingredients:

- 2 slices of bread (cubed)
- ¼ cup milk or cream
- 1 egg
- 1 teaspoon sugar
- ¼ teaspoon cinnamon
- ¼ teaspoon vanilla extract

Directions:

1. Preheat oven and spray pan with nonstick spray
2. Combine milk, egg, sugar, cinnamon and vanilla extract together in a bowl
3. Gently add in cubed bread and press down to coat
4. Let set for a couple of minutes to absorb into bread until saturated
5. Place bread into pan and gently flatten out with a fork
6. Cook for 10-13 minutes
7. Remove from oven & Sprinkle with powdered sugar

Peach Cobbler

Ingredients (makes 2 pans) :

- 2 tablespoons sugar
- 2 tablespoons all purpose flour
- ¼ teaspoon baking powder
- ½ teaspoon cinnamon
- Snack size peaches (around 6-8 total) chopped
- 1 tablespoon butter (melted)

Topping:
- Thawed whipped topping (optional)

Directions:
1. Preheat oven and spray pan with nonstick spray
2. Combine sugar, flour, baking powder, cinnamon and butter in a bowl
3. Pour into pan filling no more than halfway
4. Spoon in chopped peaches
5. Bake 10-12 minutes
6. Remove and allow to cool
7. Top with whipped topping (optional)

Cinnamon Honey Bun *(from box mix)*

Ingredients:

- 1/3 cup yellow cake mix
- 1 teaspoon finely chopped pecans
- 2 teaspoons oil
- 1 teaspoon water
- 1 egg white
- 2 teaspoons brown sugar
- ¼ teaspoon cinnamon
- 1 teaspoon finely chopped pecans

Directions:

1. Preheat oven and spray pan with nonstick spray
2. Mix together following ingredients: cake mix, pecans, oil, water, egg white
3. Poor into bottom of pan making sure not to overfill pan more than 75%
4. Sprinkle pecans, cinnamon and brown sugar on top.
5. Cook until slightly brown (10-16 minutes)
6. Remove and allow to cool

Cake Mix Brownies *(from box mix)*

Ingredients:

- 4 tablespoons chocolate cake mix
- ½ tablespoon vegetable oil
- 1 teaspoon milk
- 1 ½ teaspoons of beaten egg or applesauce
- 2 tablespoons semisweet chocolate chips

Directions:

1. Preheat oven and spray pan with nonstick spray
2. Combine all ingredients together in a bowl
3. Fill pan ½ - 2/3 full with batter
4. Bake for approximately 13-17 minutes. Don't overcook. Brownie may not appear to be done, but will continue to set up after you remove from the oven
5. Remove and allow to cool

Birthday Cake Pretzels (from frozen soft pretzels)

Ingredients:

- 1 frozen soft pretzel or pretzel nuggets
- 1 tablespoon butter (melted)
- 4 tablespoons yellow cake mix (can use white if preferred)
- Sprinkles

Directions:

1. Thaw frozen pretzel
2. Preheat oven and spray pan with nonstick spray
3. Cut pretzel into bite size pieces or cut in half horizontally so that it fits into your pan
4. In a bowl, add cut pretzel pieces and then pour melted butter over and toss gently to coat
5. Add the cake mix to pretzels and gently toss again until pretzels are coated with cake mix
6. Place the pretzels on the greased pan
7. Top pretzels with sprinkles
8. Bake for approximately 5 – 6 minutes
9. Serve warm

Pizza (from refrigerated can pizza dough)

Ingredients:

- 1 small can pizza dough
- 1 tablespoon pizza or marinara sauce
- 4 large or 8-10 mini pepperoni (optional)
- Italian herbs (basil and oregano mix)
- 1 ½ tablespoons shredded mozzarella

Directions:

1. Preheat oven and spray pan with nonstick spray
2. Roll out enough pizza dough to cover the bottom of the pan
3. Place pan with dough inside oven and precook crust for approx. 10 minutes. Crust will be slightly brown
4. Remove from oven and spread pizza sauce over crust
5. Top with mozzarella and pepperoni
6. Return to oven and cook until done (approximately 8-10 additional minutes)

Tip: Use the left over uncooked pizza dough to make the Cinnamon Dessert Pizza!

English Muffin Pizza (from store bought muffins)

Ingredients:

- 1 English muffin sliced horizontally
- 1 teaspoon olive oil (divided)
- 2 tablespoon pizza or marinara sauce (divided)
- 8-10 mini pepperoni (optional)
- Italian herbs (basil and oregano mix)
- 2 tablespoons shredded mozzarella (divided)

Directions:

1. Preheat oven and spray pan with nonstick spray
2. Place slice of English muffin on pan
3. Drizzle ½ teaspoon olive oil over English muffin
4. Spread 1 tablespoon pizza sauce or marinara over muffin
5. Top with 4-5 mini pepperoni (optional)
6. Sprinkle 1 tablespoon mozzarella cheese over muffin
7. Cook until cheese melted (approximately 10-15 minutes)
8. Remove from oven and serve immediately
9. Repeat all steps for other half of English muffin

Pizza (from scratch)

Ingredients:

- 4 tablespoons all purpose flour
- 1/8 teaspoon baking powder
- 1/16 teaspoon baking soda
- 1/8 teaspoon salt
- 3 tablespoons milk
- 1 tablespoon oil (olive is best)
- 1 tablespoon pizza or marinara sauce
- 4 large or 8-10 mini pepperoni (optional)
- Italian herbs (basil and oregano mix)
- 1 ½ tablespoons shredded mozzarella

Directions:

1. Preheat oven and spray pan with nonstick spray
2. Mix all dry ingredients together (flour, baking powder, baking soda, salt)
3. Combine milk and oil with dry ingredients to make dough
4. Place dough into pan and spread evenly
5. Spread pizza sauce or marinara over dough
6. Add pepperoni (optional)
7. Add mozzarella cheese
8. Sprinkle dried Italian herbs over pizza
9. Place in oven and cook for approximately 12-15 minutes
10. Remove from oven when done and serve immediately

Raisin Bread Pudding (from store bought raisin bread)

Ingredients:
- 2 slices raisin bread
- 2 tablespoons egg (beaten)
- ¼ cup milk
- 2 tablespoons sugar
- 1 teaspoon additional raisins (optional)

Topping:

- Cinnamon
- ½ teaspoon butter (melted)
- 1 teaspoon milk (divided)
- ¼ teaspoon sugar (optional)

Directions:

1. Preheat oven and spray pans with nonstick spray
2. Mix together egg, ¼ cup milk, 2 tablespoons sugar in a bowl
3. Break bread apart into small cubes and place into bowl. Mix well. May add additional raisins if desired.
4. Add to pan filling only ½ full. Press down using fork
5. Sprinkle cinnamon on top
6. Drizzle ½ teaspoon of milk on top
7. Drizzle ¼ teaspoon melted butter on top
8. Sprinkle light sugar on top if desired
9. Bake until golden brown (approximately 17–20 minutes)
10. Remove and serve warn

Makes two servings

Cinnamon Dessert Pizza (from frig pizza dough)

Ingredients (this makes 2 pans)

- 1small can refrigerated pizza crust dough (divided)
- 1 tablespoon butter (softened, divided)
- ½ teaspoon cinnamon (divided)
- ½ tablespoon all purpose flour
- ¾ teaspoon sugar
- 1 tablespoon brown sugar

Glaze:

- 2   tablespoons powdered sugar
- 1 ½ teaspoons milk or heavy cream
- 1/8 teaspoon vanilla extract

Directions:

1. Preheat oven and spray pans with nonstick spray
2. Roll out enough pizza dough to cover bottom of pans
3. Precook pizza dough by placing pan in over for approximately 8 minutes
4. While the crust is precooking, Mix flour, 1 teaspoon butter, ¼ teaspoon cinnamon, brown sugar and regular granulated sugar until crumbly. Set aside
5. When pizza crust has been precooked, remove from oven. Melt 1 teaspoon butter and brush over crust
6. Sprinkle ¼ teaspoon cinnamon powder over melted butter
7. Sprinkle ½ of the cinnamon crumble over the crust
8. Bake for an additional 4-6 minutes

9. While it is baking, mix all ingredients for glaze in a small bowl until blended well.
10. Spoon glaze into a sandwich bag and cut tip of corner off.
11. Remove dessert pizza from oven when ready
12. Allow to cool and then drizzle ½ glaze over pizza
13. Use remaining ingredients to make a second dessert pizza.

Cheese Bread Sticks (from refrigerated crescent rolls)

Ingredients:

- 2-4 ounces crescent rolls
- ½ teaspoon butter (melted)
- ½ teaspoon olive oil
- ¼ cup shredded cheese (cheddar or mozzarella)
- Garlic Salt

Directions:

1. Preheat oven and spray pan with nonstick spray
2. Remove crescent roll from container
3. Place two of the rectangles together and pinch in the seam to form a square
4. Flatten crescent roll into bottom of pan (remove excess)
5. Brush crescent roll with butter and olive oil
6. Sprinkle garlic salt over crescent rolls
7. Top with cheese
8. Cook until cheese melted (approximately 10 minutes)
9. Remove and cut into slices
10. Serve immediately

Frosting

Vanilla Glaze

Ingredients:

- 3 tablespoons powdered sugar
- ¾ teaspoon milk
- Pinch salt
- 1/16 teaspoon vanilla extract
- 1/8 teaspoon butter (melted)

Directions:
1. Combine all ingredients and mix until creamy

Chocolate Glaze

Ingredients:

- 3 tablespoons powdered sugar
- 3/4 teaspoon milk
- 1/4 teaspoon vanilla extract
- ½ tablespoon cocoa powder
- 1/8 teaspoon butter (melted)

Directions:
1. Combine all ingredients and mix until creamy

Peanut Butter Frosting

Ingredients:

- 3 tablespoons creamy peanut butter (do not use the natural peanut butter)
- 1/8 tablespoon unsalted butter (softened)
- 6 tablespoons powdered sugar
- 1/8 teaspoon vanilla extract
- Small pinch salt

Directions:
1. Mix all ingredients together well in a bowl

Pineapple Pudding Icing

Ingredients:

- 1 tablespoon vanilla instant pudding
- 5 tablespoons crushed pineapple with juice
- 2 tablespoons thawed whipped topping (ex. Coolwhip™)

Directions:
1. Combine pineapple and pudding mix
2. Mix in whipped topping.

Hot Chocolate Whipped Cream

Ingredients:

- ½ cup heavy whipping cream
- ¼ cup hot chocolate mix

Directions:
1. Get whisk and bowl very cold by placing in freezer for about 15-20 minutes
2. Beat heavy whipping cream for about 2 minutes
3. Add hot chocolate mix to whipped cream
4. Continue to beat until it thickens and forms a stiff peak

Lemonade Frosting

Ingredients:

- ½ tablespoon presweetened lemonade flavor drink mix
- 1 teaspoon water
- 1 tablespoon butter (softened)
- ¾ teaspoon heavy whipping cream
- 4 tablespoons powdered sugar
- Small drop yellow food color

Directions:
1. Mix all ingredients together in a bowl. Beat until light and fluffy

Lemon frosting

Ingredients:

- 6 tablespoons powdered sugar
- 1 tablespoon butter (softened)
- ¾ teaspoon lemon juice
- 1/16 teaspoon vanilla extract

Directions:

1. Combine all ingredients together and beat until light and fluffy

Unicorn Frosting

Ingredients:

- 6 tablespoons powdered sugar
- 2 tablespoon butter (softened)
- ½ tablespoon whipping cream
- 1/8 teaspoon vanilla extract
- Food coloring of choice (3 different ones)
- Edible Glitter (optional)

Directions:

1. Beat together butter and sugar until fluffy

2. Add in whipping cream and vanilla

3. Beat until light and fluffy (3-5 minutes)

4. Divide frosting into 3 smaller bowls

5. Add drop of food coloring of choice to each individual bowl (one color per bowl)

6. Mix well

7. Spoon each color into a piping bag (or use a sandwich bag with corner tip cut off if you do not have a piping bag). Try to keep each color on different sides of the bag so that they all come out together when frosting

8. Pipe frosting onto pastry item and sprinkle edible glitter on top

Vanilla Cloud Frosting

Ingredients:

- 2 tablespoons butter (softened)
- 8 tablespoons powdered sugar
- 1/8 tablespoon vanilla extract
- Tiny pinch of salt
- 1 ¼ teaspoon milk

Directions:

1. Beat butter and sugar well
2. Add vanilla
3. Mix in powdered sugar a little at a time until mixed well
4. Beat until light and fluffy

Chocolate Frosting

Ingredients:

- 2 tablespoons butter (softened)
- 1 tablespoon cocoa powder
- 10 tablespoons powdered sugar
- 1/8 teaspoon vanilla
- ½ tablespoon milk

Directions:

1. Beat butter and cocoa together until well blended
2. Add vanilla into mixture
3. Slowly add in powdered sugar
4. Slowly add in milk and beat until frosting is light and fluffy

Strawberry Buttercream

Ingredients:
- 1 ½ tablespoons butter (softened)
- 6 tablespoons powdered sugar
- 1 heaping teaspoon strawberry puree (2 strawberries pureed in a mini food processor
- ¼ teaspoon strawberry jam
- 1/16 teaspoon vanilla extract (just a couple of drops)

Directions:
1. Cream butter until creamy and smooth
2. Slowly add in powdered sugar until mixed well
3. Add in the strawberry puree, the strawberry jam and the vanilla extract. Mix well
4. Can add additional powdered sugar or strawberry puree if needed (to thin or thicken up the frosting).
5. Use a spatula or piping bag to frost your bakery items

Vanilla Buttercream Frosting

Ingredients:

- 4 tablespoons powdered sugar
- 1 tablespoon butter (softened)
- ¾ teaspoon milk
- ¼ teaspoon vanilla extract
- Food coloring of choice (optional)

Directions:

1. Cream butter until smooth (can use a wooden spoon if needed)
2. Gradually add in powdered sugar and beat together until fluffy
3. Add in vanilla and milk
4. Beat until light and fluffy (3-5 minutes)
5. Add drop of food coloring of choice to frosting
6. Mix well

Drink Mix (Kool-Aid™) Frosting

Ingredients:

- 4 tablespoons powdered sugar
- 1 tablespoon butter (softened)
- ½ tablespoon milk
- ¼ teaspoon Kool-Aid™ unsweetened drink mix
- Food coloring of choice (optional)

Directions:

1. Cream butter until smooth (can use a wooden spoon if needed)
2. Gradually add in powdered sugar and beat together until fluffy
3. Add in Kool-Aid™ and milk
4. Beat until light and fluffy (3-5 minutes)

Cake Batter Frosting

<u>Ingredients:</u>

- ¼ cup heavy whipping cream
- 1 ½ tablespoons cake mix (any flavor)
- 1 tablespoon sprinkles (optional)
- Food coloring of choice (optional)

<u>Directions:</u>

1. Using a cold bowl and whisk attachment, beat heavy whipping cream for 2 minutes
2. Add in cake mix and beat until thick and stiff peak is visible
3. Add in drop of food coloring and sprinkles if desired. Mix well

Cream Cheese Frosting

Ingredients:

- 1 tablespoon unsalted butter (softened)
- 1 ounce cream cheese (softened)
- 1/8 teaspoon vanilla extract
- Pinch salt
- 8 tablespoons powdered sugar

Directions:

1. Cream together butter and cream cheese until smooth
2. Add in salt and vanilla extract
3. Slowly add in powdered sugar until mixed well

My Favorite Recipes:

My Favorite Recipes:

My Favorite Recipes:

Can you please do the Hasty Tasty Chef a huge favor?
(because we could sure use your help)

Would you please go to Amazon.com really quick and leave a review for this book? We really do need people like you to go and share your thoughts about our book by leaving a review. It helps us more than you can imagine.

I certainly hope that you have found the recipes helpful. We would love to see a picture of your creations! And we've got some we want to share with you!

Don't forget to find The Hasty Tasty Chef on Facebook and join in on all the fun today!